# Contents

## KNITTING TERMS & ABBREVIATIONS

| | | | |
|---|---|---|---|
| approx | approximate | p | purl |
| beg | begin(ning) | p2tog | purl two together |
| BO | bind off | PM | place marker |
| CC | contrasting color | psso | past slip stitch over |
| CO | cast on | PU | pick up |
| cont | continue | RF | right front |
| dec | decrease | rem | remaining |
| dpn | double-pointed needles | RS | right side |
| inc | increase | sl | slip |
| k | knit | sl m | slip marker |
| k2tog | knit two together | ssk | slip, slip, knit two stitches together |
| k2tog tbl | knit two together through back loops | st(s) | stitch(es) |
| | | St st | stockinette stitch |
| LF | left front | tog | together |
| M1 | make one | WS | wrong side |
| M2 | make two | wyib | with yarn in back |
| MC | main color | wyif | with yarn in front |
| m | meter | yo | yarn over |

# STRIPES

A fun, exciting, and simple way to add color to
your knitting is to use stripes. Stripes can be as simple as a
two color repeat or as complex as changing colors every row.
Stripes can be made in stockinette stitch or in patterned
stitches, the choice is up to you.

# Techniques

Although striping seems pretty straightforward—changing yarn colors between rows or rounds—there are methods and tricks to perfect those color changes and to make them as inconspicuous as possible. Striping techniques for knitting back and forth on two needles are different from those used when knitting circularly. There are advantages and disadvantages to both. How you make the color changes and what you do with the yarn when it's not in use make a big difference in the quality of the finished fabric.

## CHANGING COLORS WHEN WORKING FLAT
When working back and forth in rows, there are a few things to master when it comes to changing colors.

### Back and Forth on Two Needles
You are ready to start your new color on the right edge of your knitting. Drop your old color and start knitting with your new color. The first thing you might notice is the edge gets a bit sloppy. You can put a temporary knot on the edge with the old and new colors together, then later when sewing up your seams you can unknot and work them in or use them to sew up your side seams.

## Carry Yarn

If you were to cut each time you changed colors, you would have many ends to deal with. A neater finish is to carry your yarn up the edge. When carrying up the edge, be careful not to pull up too tightly or the edge of your knitting will pucker and be shorter and less elastic. Carry yarns about three or four rows. If the stripe is wider than that, either cut the yarn or catch the carried yarn with your working yarn at the edge. This can be done by twisting the carried yarn; to do this at the edge, lift the carried yarn up and over the working yarn and knit the edge stitch. This will lock it into the edge.

▲ Locking the edge: The brown yarn is dropped to the right and the next color in the sequence, orange, is picked up from behind. Knit across with orange. Note at the edge the twist that is formed when the colors are locked.

## Back and Forth on a Circular Needle

Another way to knit stripes back and forth is to use a circular needle to knit back and forth as if you were using straight needles. Sometimes your stripe sequence will end at the opposite side of where you just ended working your row. Since you are on a circular needle, all you need to do is to slide your stitches along the cable and begin knitting again from the other end of your needle. This is especially easy if you are working stockinette stitch (knit on the right side and purl on the wrong side) and works great if you are working an odd number of rows.

▼ Notice that the row just finished is white and has ended on the left. If you were to continue knitting with white, you would turn your knitting and purl across the back. But the next row of pattern is warm brown and that color ended at the opposite side. Since you are working on circular needles, slide the work to the other end of the needle and knit across with warm brown.

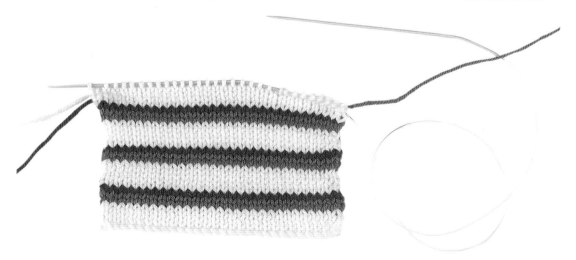

# CIRCULAR KNITTING

The advantages of knitting in the round are color changes all occur at the starting point of the rounds, and if it's a garment, there are no side seams to sew. The disadvantage is at the start point you will get a jog in your knitting when changing colors. When you knit back and forth, each row is completed and the next row is directly above it. When you knit circularly, you are making a spiral, so the ends of the rounds don't meet but rather continue one stitch higher. There are a few techniques to minimize the jog. If the jog occurs at the side seam of a garment sometimes it is easiest to ignore it. Decide how much the jog offends you. If you are using finer yarn the jog will be less noticeable compared to a bulkier yarn.

▲ Jog that occurs in circular knitting.

These notes refer to all jog fixes:

*Note:* All jog fix instructions use a marker for reference to the actions taken, always marking the beginning of the round.

*Note:* Because color changes are all happening on top of each other, there will be loose yarns on the wrong side of the fabric and it will look sloppy. When all your yarns are worked in and finished off, the area will neaten.

## Jog Fix #1

This fix needs two or more rounds to use.

▲ Jog Fix #1.
The lifted and first stitch knit together highlighted.

*1.* Work one row of new color, slip marker. Lift the back of the stitch from the row below and place on left-hand needle.

*1*

**2.** Knit the first and lifted stitch together.

The disadvantage to this technique is the beginning of each round is one stitch height shorter than the rest. This is only a problem if there are many stripes because losing a stitch height at this point repeatedly, can cause the fabric to draw down or pucker over a larger area. This is a nice fix to use if your stripes are further apart and happen less frequently.

2

## Jog Fix #2

*1.* *Work one round of new color. At the start of the next round, remove the marker from the needle, slip the first stitch, and replace the marker after the slip stitch.
*2.* Knit desired rounds. Repeat from *.

The advantage to this fix is all the rows stay the same height. The disadvantage is with every color change the start of the row moves over one to the left. This can cause a slight spiral, and if you have many stripes, the start point could move to an undesirable area, such as the front of a hat.

▲ Jog Fix #2.
Slip stitch highlighted.

## Jog Fix #3

This jog fix is the same as Jog Fix #2 except do not move your marker one to the left.

The advantage of this fix is the color change remains in the same place. The disadvantage is similar to Jog Fix #1, you lose one row on that first slipped stitch and the fabric will draw down slightly. If you have many stripes, this could shorten or pucker at this point.

▲ Jog Fix #3.
Slip stitch highlighted.

## Jog Fix #4

I discovered this fix, and made up my own variation, similar to Jog Fix #2. As long as the start of your next color change row does not fall on top of the start of the previous color by 2 stitches (or more), you will not form a spiral. In order not to jog, start your color changes at different points on your knitting, forward and backward.

Within your color block area you will have spiraling, but since it's in the same color, you will not see it.

Your marker does not move, but the beginning of your round does. No matter where the first stitch starts, say two stitches after the marker, when

▲ Jog Fix #4.
The first stitch of each color change is highlighted.

the rounds of striping are done, it will need to end two stitches after the marker, thus making a complete round.

*1.* Knit to the point where you want to change colors, ending at the marker. Slip the marker and the next two stitches. This becomes your new start point, two stitches past the marker.

*Note:* You could add a second different colored marker to use as you move your beginning points around and keep your original marker to mark your "true" starting point.

*2.* With new color, knit the required number of rounds, ending at your new start point. (2 sts past the marker).

**3.** Slip two stitches from right needle back to left needle, you will be back at your marker. The new color can start here at marker or slip the marker and the next two stitches from the right needle back to the left needle and knit the required rounds with the new color at its new starting point.

**4.** Continue in this manner moving your starting point around. It doesn't matter if you slip 2, 3, or 4 stitches (don't do less than 2), only that you complete your rounds and move your starting points around.

3

If your stripes are narrow and you want to carry the yarns up rather than cut them, you must carry the yarn straight up or to the left. Carrying a yarn to the right will create a small hole.

An advantage to moving two stitches is the start points do not all line up, which makes for easier color changes with all the loose ends not occurring directly on top of each other. The rounds stay the same height and the starts are not on top of each other, making for a bit easier knitting. The disadvantage, as with all fixes, is that you see a slight dip where the colors change, but with this technique the dip is very slight.

## STRIPED RIBS

When making ribs with color stripes a dot from the preceding color will show up on your purled stitches. This could be considered a design choice or an untidy dot. If you do not like the dot it is easily eliminated by knitting the first row of the color change, assuming you have three or more rows to your color stripe. Then continue with your ribbing pattern, as in this case a knit two, purl two. This one row of knit (or purl if your color change occurs on the wrong side) will not change your amount of elasticity and will eliminate the dot.

# Striped Stitch Patterns

The following five stripe patterns will provide good practice in changing colors. With the aid of the chart, you can convert to knitting in the round by changing the even numbered rows. On the even numbered rows the knits become purls and purls become knits. The first two patterns are easily converted, but the last three are a bit more challenging. Remember to work the opposite; as in the Daisy Stitch, instead of p3tog, it becomes a k3tog.

## BASIC STRIPE

Basic stripes can be dramatic. This sample, if knit flat, should still be done on circular needles because the stripe has odd numbered repeats. Some color changes will occur on the opposite side of where your row just ended. Just slide the stitches to the other end of the cable and continuing in stockinette stitch with the new color.

*Worked on any number of sts.*
*Four colors: A, B, C, and D.*
*Follow chart for color changes.*

= A
= B  } K on RS
= C  } P on WS
= D

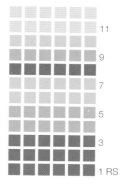

## TEXTURED STRIPE

As when making ribs, when you change colors you will need to make one row in knit so you will not have a 'dot' from the previous row. Look closely at the chart, and you can see there is a knit row at each color change. You do not notice this row in the knitted swatch as the purl bumps lay on top of the knit row.

*Multiple of 2 sts.*
*Three colors: A, B, and C.*
*Follow chart for color changes.*

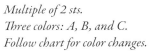

■ = A
■ = B
□ = C

⊟ = P on RS, K on WS
☐ = K on RS, P on WS

repeat

# DAISY STITCH (STAR STITCH)

This cute pattern can be used to make a two-color stripe pattern but can also be used to make stripes with as many color changes as desired. Colors can be changed every two rows.

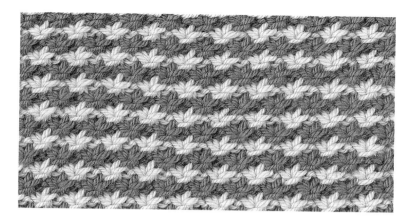

*Multiple of 4 sts plus 1.*
*Two colors: A and B or three colors;*
*A, B, and C.*

Make star: p3tog leaving sts on needle, yo, p3tog again.

Row 1 (RS): With A, knit.

Row 2: With A, k1, *make star, k1; repeat from * to end.

Row 3: With B, knit.

Row 4: With B, k1, p1, k1, *make star, k1; repeat from *, end p1, k1.

Repeat rows 1-4.

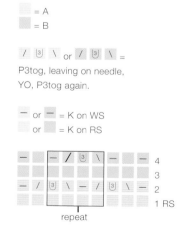

☐ = A

☐ = B

/ ③ \ or / ③ \ =
P3tog, leaving on needle,
YO, P3tog again.

— or — = K on WS
☐ or ☐ = K on RS

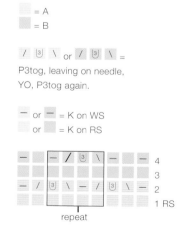

repeat

# LITTLE CROWNS

This pattern has a similar feel to Daisy Stitch, but incorporates yarn-overs and the (k1, p1, k1) move is made on the right side of the fabric. Garter stitch separates the crown rows.

*Multiple of 3 sts plus 2.*
*Three colors: A, B, and C.*

Row 1 (RS): With A, knit.

Row 2: With A, knit.

Row 3: With B, k1, knit to last st wrapping yarn twice around needle for each st, end k1.

Row 4: With B, k1, *slip next 3 sts to RH needle dropping extra loops, slip these 3 sts back to LH needle, k1, p1, k1 through 3 sts tog: repeat from *, end k1.

Rows 5 & 6: Same as rows 1 & 2.

Row 7 & 8: With C, same as rows 3 & 4.

Repeat rows 1-8 for repeat.

■ = A

■ = B

■ = C

●■■■● or ●■■■● = pass 3 sts to RH needle dropping extra loops, pass back to LH needle, K1, P1, K1 through 3 sts together.

|2| or |2| = K wrapping yarn twice over needle.

■ = K on RS, — = K on WS

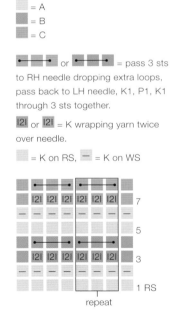

# GRANITE RELIEF STITCH

Four rows make up each color stripe in this pattern. This swatch uses 4 colors; any number of color changes can be used, as few as 2 or as many colors as you have. Rows will have different row counts because of rapid deceases and increases in rows 2 and 3.

*Multiple of 2.*
*Four colors: A, B, C, and D.*

Row 1 (RS): With A knit.

Row 2: With A, k2tog across.

Row 3: With A, k into the front and back of each st.

Row 4: With A, purl.

Repeat these 4 rows changing colors as desired.

V = K into front and back of stitch

Δ = K2 tog WS

= K on RS, P on WS

# SLIP STITCH & MOSAIC

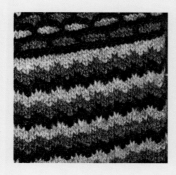  

An easy way to add beautiful color to your knitting is to
use slip stitch patterns and mosaic stitch patterns. These patterns
can be very simple to make and are very effective in producing
a lovely ornamented fabric.

# Techniques

Looking complicated but easy to execute, slip stitch and mosaic patterns use only one yarn or color per row. They produce a fabric that is dense and is tightly knit because the stitch is pulled up and is knit in the following row or even stretched over several rows. This can make the fabric less elastic, so using a bigger needle can help relax this tendency. A fine or soft yarn is also a good choice for these patterns. The natural tendencies of this type of stitch make them perfect for outerwear like hats, mittens, and jackets. They are also strong, which makes them equally good for purses, bags, and similar items.

## SLIP STITCH

There are two main concerns with slipping stitches. The first is which way to insert the needle; purlwise or knitwise. The standard practice is to insert your needle purlwise unless the pattern specifically tells you to do the opposite. This way, the stitch is oriented correctly on the needle, ready to be knit or purled on the next row. If you slip knitwise, your stitch will be twisted. You should slip purlwise whether you are on the right side or wrong side of your work unless your pattern instructs otherwise.

The second concern is where the working yarn is held, in front as if to purl or in back as if to knit. It could be in either position, all depending on the pattern. So if the instructions do not specify, your yarn will be held toward the wrong side of your fabric. So when working on the right side, your yarn is held behind the needles, also known as "with yarn in back" (abbreviated as wyib). On the wrong side of your work the yarn is held in front of the needles or "with yarn in front" (abbreviated as wyif).

▲ Slipping your stitch purlwise

▲ Slipping stitches with yarn in back

▲ Slipping stitches with yarn in front

# MOSAIC

Mosaic patterns are made with slip stitches and use one color per two rows. Therefore mosaic patterns change colors on every right side row, so the same colored yarn is always used in two row increments. Mosaic knitting can be either a garter stitch base or stockinette stitch base. Garter stitch mosaics are condensed and the motifs have a framed feel. Stockinette stitch mosaics, while still dense, do not have as thick of an appearance and can look more like stranded knitting. On the stockinette base the stitches that are slipped often look distorted, but a good blocking will smooth out its appearance. The same is true for a garter stitch base, but the stockinette base shows the distortion more. Like regular slip stitches, all stitches are slipped purlwise and the working yarn is held toward the wrong side of the work.

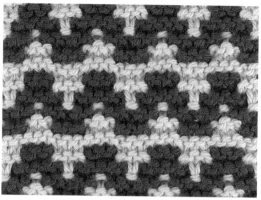

▲ Garter Stitch Base

▲ Stockinette Stitch Base

## Charting Mosaics

There are two ways mosaics are charted. The first is used by Barbara G. Walker. In her books one row of the chart equals two knit rows. Second is when all rows are shown in the chart, as would be typical of most, if not all other types of knitting charts. I prefer Barbara G. Walker's method because the chart more closely resembles the finished work and with a regular chart it is redundant to show identical rows.

Since I am using Barbara G. Walker's charting method, looking at the chart, you will see that all rows are numbered on both sides and that one row of the chart represents two rows of knitting. Like all charts, you start at the bottom right corner and read the first row to the left. When coming back on the return row you do not even need to refer to the chart. Knit (for a garter base) the stitches you have knit and slip the stitches you have just slipped, meaning the same stitches are being worked and slipped as in the first row. If you want your design to have a stockinette base, you would purl the stitches on the return row and slip the stitches you have just slipped. Now you are back to the right side ready to start the third row color changes. You will drop the first color and pick up your second color and work two rows, continuing to alternate. To make a neat edge where the colors change, hold the yarn just worked to the right, pick up the new color from underneath, and work your next row.

On the chart, you will also notice the first and last vertical edges have alternating colors. Whatever color is on the edge, is the color you will be working across on that row. For example, if black is the edge color in the graph, then on this row you will be

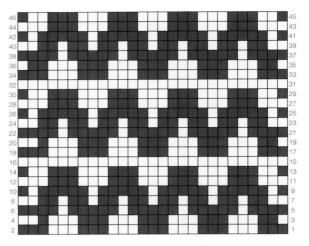

A. Barbara G. Walker's charting method. Note: the numbering of rows, one row of the chart equals two rows of knitting.

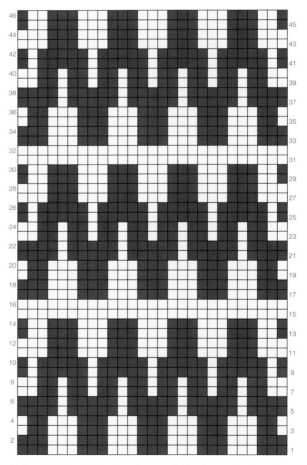

B. Regular Chart showing all rows. Note: the numbering of rows reflecting the right side and wrong side of knitting.

knitting the black stitches and slipping the white. Your cast on edge must be "white," the opposite color of the first edge stitch which is "black" or your first row will not have color changes. I will refer to all colors as black and white in the following instructions, but of course the sky's the limit to what colors you chose for your project.

## Working through the chart

Referring to the mosaic chart A, it begins and ends with a black square in row 1. You will start by knitting the black square and continue reading the row to the left, knitting the black squares and slipping the white squares. Row 2 is the same: knit (or purl for stockinette stitched fabric) the black squares and slip the white squares. Right side facing, drop the black yarn towards the right and pick up the white yarn from underneath. Leave the black yarn hanging. For the next row the operation changes. Row 3 starts with a white square, so now you work the opposite; you will knit the white squares and slip the black squares. Row 4 is the same as row 3, knitting the white squares, slipping the black squares. Row 5 starts with a black square so you will reverse again and knit with the black squares and slip with the white

squares, continuing on in this way. If you come across a row that is all black or white, knit the whole row and returning row. There will be no slipped stitches on such rows.

## Mosaic in the round

Cast on the amount of stitches needed for the multiple minus the edge stitches. Round one would be the same as in flat knitting; knit the black stitches and slip the white. Round two will continue the same as round one, purling the black stitches for a garter stitch fabric or knitting for a stockinette stitch fabric and slipping (with yarn behind) the white stitches. Round three will start with the white stitches being knit and the black stitches being slipped. Round four will be either a knit or purl row, depending on your choice of garter or stockinette stitch base as established and slipping the black stitches. Continue on with one color per two rows and in garter stitch or stockinette base.

When changing colors, pick up your new color to the left of the old and you will create a spiral. You can also pick up to the right, just be consistent with your choice and a spiral will form and keep the inside looking nice.

# Slip Stitch & Mosaic Pattern Samples

The first three patterns in this section are a sampling of slip stitches. The last two patterns are mosaic patterns—one a garter stitch base and the other a stockinette stitch base.

### RIC-RAC PATTERN

This simple slip stitch pattern is shown in two colors but would be very beautiful using three, four, or many multiples of colors. Every two rows the colors can be changed. This pattern can have the appearance of ribbing especially if a light hand is used in the blocking.

*Odd Number of Stitches.*
*Two colors: A and B.*

Row 1 (WS): With A, purl.

Row 2: With B, k1,*sl 1, k1; repeat from *.

Row 3: With B, purl.

Row 4: With A, k1, *sl 1, k1; repeat from*.

Row 5: With A, purl.

Repeat from row 2.

### Ric-Rac Chart

Color A — K on RS, P on WS

— Slip St.
Color B — K on RS, P on WS
— Slip St.

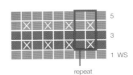

# CHECK PATTERN

This cute check has the appearance of stranded knitting. The first row of this pattern has a straight row of color A, and looking at the swatch you might think this is a mistake, but A is the color that gets slipped and pulls over colors B and C.

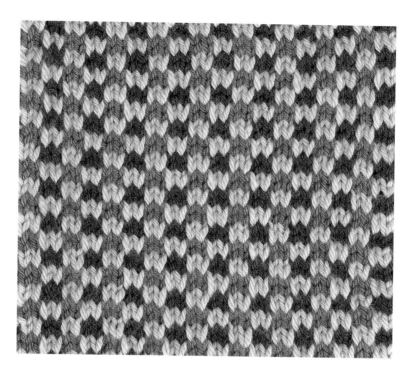

*Multiple of 4 sts plus 2.*
*Three colors: A, B, and C.*

Row 1(RS): With A, knit.

Row 2: With B, p1, *sl 2, p2; repeat from *, end p1.

Row 3: With B, k3, sl 2, *k2, sl 2 repeat from*, end k1.

Row 4: With A, purl.

Row 5: With C, k1, *sl 2, k2; repeat from *, end k1.

Row 6: With C, p3, sl 2, *p2, sl 2; repeat from *, end p1.

Repeat rows 1-6.

## Check Pattern Chart

| Color A | | K on RS, P on WS |
| Color B | | K on RS, P on WS |
| | X | Slip St. |
| Color C | | K on RS, P on WS |
| | X | Slip St. |

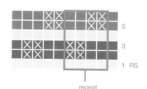

repeat

# BLACK FOREST PATTERN

This pretty slip stitch has the added texture of a purl row. A very simple pattern to knit with a design that looks very complex.

*Multiple of 4 sts plus 3.*
*Three colors: A, B, and C.*

Row 1(RS): With A, knit.

Row 2: With A, purl.

Row 3: With B, k3, *sl 1, k3; repeat from *.

Row 4: With B, p3, *sl 1, p3: repeat from *.

Row 5: With C, k1, *sl 1, k3; repeat from *, end sl 1, k1.

Row 6: With C, k1, *sl 1, k3: repeat from *, end sl 1, k1.

Rows 7 and 8: With B, repeat rows 3 and 4.

Row 9: With A, repeat row 5.

Row 10: With A, p1, *sl 1, p3; repeat from *, end sl 1, p1.

Repeat rows 1-10.

## Black Forest Chart

| Color A | K on RS, P on WS |
| | Slip St. |
| Color B | K on RS, P on WS |
| | Slip St. |
| Color C | K on RS, P on WS |
| | Slip St. |
| | P on RS, K on WS |

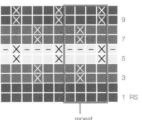

repeat

## TREND MOSAIC

This handsome strong geometric pattern is made with a garter stitch base, so the wrong side rows are knit. This pattern could also be made with a stockinette base by changing the wrong side rows to purl. Follow instructions for mosaic knitting on pages 19 to 21.

*Multiple of 18 sts plus 2 edge sts.*
*Two colors: A and B.*
Follow chart.

### Trend Mosaic Chart

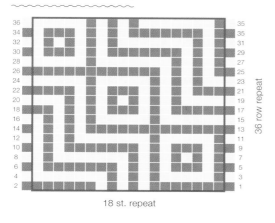

18 st. repeat

## FLORENTINE MOSAIC

A beautiful zigzag pattern based on a background of stockinette gives this pattern a stranded knit appearance. By changing the wrong side rows from a purl to a knit, the base fabric becomes garter stitched and would be equally nice. Follow instructions for mosaic knitting on pages 19 to 21.

*Multiple of 21 sts plus 2 edge sts.*
*Two colors: A and B.*
Follow chart.

### Florentine Mosaic Chart

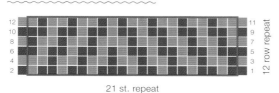

21 st. repeat

# Striped Zigzag Scarf

A new twist to a traditional pattern, this exciting zigzag scarf is knit with one variegated and four solid colored yarns. The scarf is knit on the long edge, requiring you to cast on a large number of stitches. To make the cast-on easier, add markers every 50 stitches to aid in counting. You must use a circular knitting needle with a long cable to comfortably accommodate all the stitches.

## MATERIALS

#2 Fine wool-blend yarn; 191 yd (175 m) each of a variegated yarn (A), and four solid colors (B), (C), (D), and (E)

Size 4 (3.5 mm) 29" (74 cm) circular needles or size to obtain gauge

## Gauge

30 sts and 8 rows = 4" (10 cm) in Zigzag pattern on size 4 (3.5 mm) needles

## Finished Measurements

5½" (14 cm) wide by 62" (155 cm) long

## Row Patterns

RSP (Right Side Purl): k1, ssk *p9, sl 2, k1, p2sso; repeat from *, end p9, k2tog, k1.

RSK (Right Side Knit): k1, ssk *k9, sl 2, k1, p2sso; repeat from *, end k9, k2tog, k1.

WSP (Wrong Side Purl): k1, p5 *(p1, yo, p1 in next st), p9; repeat from *, end (p1, yo, p1 in next st), p5, k1.

## Instructions

With B, cable CO 459 sts.

Row 1 (RS): With B, RSP.

Row 2: With C, WSP.

Row 3: With C, RSK.

Row 4: With A. WSP.

Row 5: With A, RSP.

Row 6: With A, WSP.

Row 7: With A, RSP.

Row 8: With A, WSP.

Row 9: With A, RSK.

Row 10: With D, WSP.

Row 11: With D, RSP.

Row 12: With E, WSP.

Row 13: With E, RSK.

Row 14: With B, WSP.

Repeat rows 1-14 two more times (a total of 3 repeats).

End: With B, BO in pattern RSP.

# Mosaic Wristlets

Warm and soft, this wristlet is sure to be a hit. Knit flat and sewn for easy construction. Finish the edges with a crocheted picot, which adds femininity to the design.

## MATERIALS

#2 Sport weight yarn; 110 yds (100 m) each of brown (A) and blue (B)

Size 4 (3.50 mm) needles or size to obtain gauge

Size D/3 (3.25 mm) crochet hook

Tapestry needle

## Gauge

23 sts and 28 rows = 4" (10 cm) in Mosaic Stitch on size 4 (3.50 mm) needles

## Finished Measurements

6½" (17 cm) high by 7¾" (19.5 cm) around wrist

## Mosaic Wristlet Chart

Note: Every row of chart represents 2 rows. Refer to pages 31–32 for instructions on how to knit garter stitch mosaic.

■ = A
■ = B

With A, Cable CO 44 sts. Follow chart for pattern and color changes. BO in A on row 87. Block and sew seam to form a tube. With crochet hook and A, make a picot edge as follows: starting at top seam *chain 3, sl stitch twice*; repeat to end. Make matching picot on bottom edge. Make second wristlet.

# Slip Stitch Purse

Fast and simple, this purse is made with three colors using two different slip stitch motifs. A picot edge and I-cord strap finish it off in a cinch. To construct this purse, knit one side then pick up stitches from the bottom and work the second side. If you use a traditional cable cast on, there will be a slight ridge defining the bottom of the finished purse. Another choice is to use a provisional cast on (page 140) which provides live stitches to pick up, resulting in a smooth transition from one side to the other. If you use the provisional cast on, when you pick up your live stitches to work the second side of the purse, you will be one stitch short, so on that first row of the second side you will need to increase one stitch.

## MATERIALS

#4 Worsted weight wool; 190 yds (173 m) each of black (A), medium gray (B), and light gray (C)

Size 6 (4.0 mm) needles straights and double points or size to obtain gauge

Size 5 (3.75 mm) needles or size to obtain gauge

Size 4 (3.50 mm) needles or size to obtain gauge

### Gauge

22 sts and 37 rows = 4" (10 cm) over bottom half of purse Slip Stitch pattern with size 6 (4.00 mm) needle

### Finished Measurements

8" (20.5 cm) high × 7" (18 cm) wide

*Note:* This pattern calls for three different needle sizes: one for the body of the purse, and two for the final five rows of the picot edge. The first three rows of the last five rows are worked with size 5 (3.75 mm) needles and the final two rows are worked with size 4 (3.50 mm) needles. Using the smaller size 4 (3.50 mm) needles will help make the inside hem circumference slightly smaller than the outside, giving you a well formed final picot hem.

### Purse

With size 6 (4.00 mm) needles and A, Cable CO 37 sts.

Follow chart (page 32) for pattern, color, and needle changes to make the first side.

To make the second side, turn upside down, either PU 37 sts if you used a traditional CO, or if using the provisional CO, release the waste yarn and PU the 36 live sts, remembering to increase one stitch on the following row. Follow chart for second side.

Sew side seams. Fold top edge at the yo, k2tog row to make a picot top, sew down on the inside.

### Strap

With size 6 (4.00 mm) needles and A, CO 3 sts and make I-cord for 52" (132 cm). Weave straps through holes as pictured. Graft two ends together.

Change to size 4 needles–

Change to size 5 needles–

## Slip Stitch Purse

Note: on rows 53-54 and
69-70 the slip stitch is only
2 rows; all others are 4 rows

■ = A
■ = B
□ = C

M = Cable CO
B = BO
O = YO
\ = SSK
/ = K2tog
X = Slip st
□ = K on RS, P on WS
☒ = Slip st
■ = K on RS, P on WS
⊟ = K on WS
☒ = Slip st
■ = K on RS, P on WS
◣ = SSK
◪ = K2tog

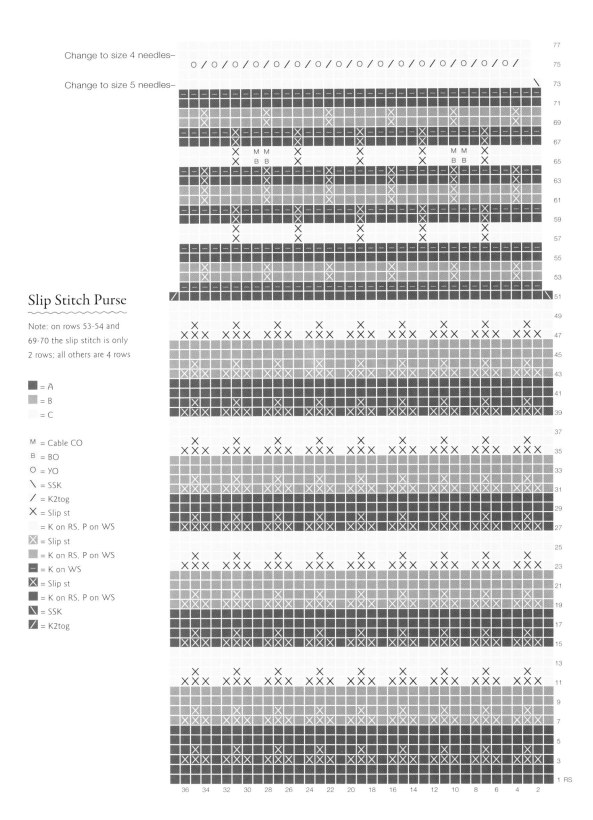